GETTING TO FIRST BASE

The Art of the Pitch

@thatwritingchic

Words To Live By Publishing
P O Box 7056
West Orange, NJ 07052
www.thatwritingchic.com

Publisher's Note: Disclaimer: The mention of any entity within this document does not imply ownership or affiliation of any kind or that the author is holder of any copyright with respect to any business noted. No copyright infringement is intended.

Book Layout © 2014 BookDesignTemplates.com
Cover Design: Donnell Sainvil
Edited by: Lady Blogga

Getting To First Base: The Art of the Pitch -- 1st Ed.
ISBN 978-0-9960129-7-3

DEDICATION/THANKS

This book is dedicated to Valerie Elustondo. Val, thanks for tirelessly listening to my pitches and helping me to examine my creative process more closely, always reminding me that it takes more than a great idea to make things happen.

Special thanks to my favorite daughter Ashley and my favorite son Khaleel. Being a child of a self proclaimed ADD creative is not always easy. I am honored that God gifted you to me and entrusted me to be your mom. Even in the toughest of times, you were and continue to be the greatest loves of my life.

Thanks to John E. Johnson for believing in me, for encouraging me and for seeing value in me during the time of my greatest insecurity. I'm certain you are in heaven orchestrating some of the greatest productions known to man.

Thanks to Laverne Hines-Moore for being one of my greatest cheerleaders and to Stacey Alston for being a constant reader of whatever I write. Quantet Walker, you are my ROCK. I appreciate you more than words can express and am blessed to call each of you friend. You are my sisters for life.

CONTENTS

INTRODUCTION

GETTING TO FIRST BASE

Many people subscribe to the belief that "Luck is what happens when preparation meets opportunity". The quote and the thinking behind it attributed to the Roman philosopher Seneca, is an oxymoron.

The purpose of preparation is to ensure that you are ready when opportunities present themselves. Who invests time, energy and effort merely hoping to merely be lucky enough for an opportunity to randomly appear?

In order for an opportunity to manifest into a reality, we need to make sure we are prepared each step of the way.

Just as we'd like to think that first impressions are lasting upon those whom we meet, so is our first pitch.

Our first pitch is the introduction of our skills, our ideas and our goals.

While I am speaking from my experiences as an entertainment industry veteran, these principles can readily be applied to your first interview with a new company for a new job and your first meeting with a new mentor. Throughout the years I have come to value process. No one wakes up one day with a blockbuster movie or Emmy Award winning television show. We live in a microwave culture where there seems to be a 'quick and dirty' way to get things done. Although some of the steps contained in this book may feel tedious, they are well worth the effort and have a significant impact upon your desired results.

I had no intentions of writing this book. The other two books in this series: "Opening Doors: Getting Connected" and "Breaking Into Television: An Insider's Guide" were written in response to questions I received on social media as I would post about my career trajectory. This book is different.

While I was working at Iconic TV, a company that is a part of YouTube's Premium Content Initiative, I wanted to make sure that I taught my interns something valuable. I realized that many of them would be attending a pitch day as part of their internship program, but I also wanted to convey information that would help them far beyond their experiences with me. As many of them would be looking for a job upon graduation, I decided to present the information in a way that would benefit them in the job search process as well.

I prepared a "simple" outline with four headings, which included five tips under each. It was well received and I made a decision to write and self-publish an e-book. This is an expanded version of that endeavor.

Pitching is something we do every day of our lives. We pitch ourselves to prospective clients, employers and even dates. No matter whom you are seeking to leave a positive lasting impression upon, the principles are the same across the board.

For anyone who wants to make sure that you get to first base safely and continue through the process to make a home run, the time, energy and effort invested will yield worthwhile results.

As in the game of baseball, not every pitch results in a home run. But, that doesn't stop the flow of the game and neither should you become so discouraged after a pitch that you give up pursuing your objective.

Some sections are followed by a "To Do" list of exercises for you to complete before moving to the next phase in the process. They are designed to measure just how serious you are about getting the results you desire. Please don't take them lightly.

Let's get started.

5 THINGS TO DO BEFORE A PITCH

While there are many things to keep in mind that will move you ahead of others who may be competing with you, this book is comprised of the things that I have found to be consistent in each of my areas of expertise and among those who have been success in my field.

Even before you set up your meeting, your interview or chat with someone who holds the key to your success, you should equip yourself properly to make sure that your first meeting is not your last.

Let's begin with the 5 things you should do before you even set up your meeting.

1. Define Your Idea

If you don't know what you are talking about, you cannot express it to others much less expect them to understand your concept.

Take the time to create a logline - two to three sentences to sum up your idea. If you are interviewing for a job, what is your career objective?

I once read a synopsis (summary) for a screenplay that to my horror, felt incredibly like a series of books that I have been working on for several years. Once I read the screenplay, the execution was nothing like my storyline at all.

Make sure that you can give the listener a clear visual picture of your carefully crafted concept.

Remember that the only thing that separates your idea from those that are similar is the execution. If it is a television show, what does an episode look like? What is the overall problem and how does it get resolved? Be as specific as possible so that you stand out among the masses.

Taking the time to define your idea will help you get closer to your project and enable you to speak about it with conviction, authority and passion.

Prepare a full treatment – a detailed breakdown of your television show or screenplay. In the case of a series, the treatment should give specifics about the entire season and explain what happens in each episode. Your screenplay treatment should tell a story, including only major points that move the script forward.

For your meeting, you may only get to speak about your pitch or share details based upon your one-sheet. A one-sheet includes all of the major details about your project. It should include your logline, an episode summary, if a television show, and details such as the number of episodes and the budget for each episode in addition to the length of each episode. Note all talent involved, distinguishing if they have signed onto the project or they are on your wish list.

An excellent resource on formatting is David Trottier's book, "The Screenwriter's Bible: A Complete Guide to Writing, Formatting and Selling Your Script."

Keep in mind that creative people like visuals. Don't go overboard, but make sure to use appropriate pictures in a presentation so that you will have something to leave behind if need be.

Taking the time to define your idea will help you get closer to your project and enable you to speak about it with conviction, authority and passion.

In the case of television, if you plan on pitching to more than one Production Company or network, you should prepare more than one version of your pitch. Although the concept will remain the same, the execution may need to change based on the person and organization you are pitching to. Keep your targeted demo in mind for each pitch and include why your project would be a fit for that market.

To Do

Describe your concept below in two to three sentences. If you are going on a job interview, describe your career objective. Develop three different versions to ensure you are stating the concept as clearly and concisely as possible. Sometimes it helps to step away for a while and then come back and refine what you have written.

Pitch 1:

Pitch 2:

Pitch 3:

Pitch before your family and friends. Ask them if they have questions when you are done. If they do, you have not clearly defined your idea. Write down any criticisms received and adjust your pitch as necessary.

2. Protect Your Concept

If you don't take anything else away from this book, please remember these words:

You CANNOT protect an IDEA. You can only protect the EXECUTION. To say that you are pitching a music show in which contestants get eliminated each week is an idea that is broad and vague.

Use a more detailed approach for the pitch. You might say that you are pitching a music show in which each performer competes for a chance to be mentored in a group by a music industry executive. The finalist will secure a record deal with a specific production company. This more detailed explanation speaks about the execution of the idea and more clearly defines how your show differs from others that may currently be in production.

Contrary to what most people think, there aren't too many truly original ideas. The execution is what will set you apart from others who may be pitching a similar idea.

Lay out specifics about what happens during each episode throughout the entire season. Those details are what make the project yours.

If it's a movie, create character sketches that define the background of each of the major players in the film and how their story lines evolve within each act of the script.

You CANNOT protect an IDEA. You can only protect the EXECUTION.

Over the years, I have heard many people say that they are afraid to share their ideas because they may get stolen. Each time my response has been:

- Protect your work.
- If you think that someone has stolen your idea, and you have a VALID claim, let him or her do all the work of making the money. Then sue them to get your fair share.
- Everyone has ideas. It is the execution that matters most.

The truth is that there is a great chance that someone, somewhere has an idea very similar to yours. When I worked at MTV I pitched several shows, but one in particular involved a DJ competition. As I spelled out what I thought was my unique execution, I was told that at least seven people had that same pitch.

Three years later, I attached a songwriter to my pitch. She had been writing many of the songs that were at the top of the music charts, while simultaneously appearing on at least two television shows. When we took the "new and improved" pitch to the head of a powerful production company that had a relationship with a different network that we wanted to pitch it to, would you believe that the Executive had a VERY similar pitch and pulled out the pitch deck as I was sharing my vision with him?

Take the time to fill out the appropriate Copyright forms and in the least, register your treatment with the Writer's Guild. The Writer's Guild will provide you with proof of registration much sooner than the U.S. Copyright office. Both registrations can be completed on their website for a nominal fee.

Many years ago, people were big fans of "the poor man's copyright." It involved mailing yourself a copy of your music, idea, writing, etc. via certified mail so that the date stamp would be created. The idea was to keep the envelope sealed and "break open in case of emergency" - meaning only open if the need arose to prove that you were the original copyright owner.

Most of the work you create can be protected for a $35 fee. If you are not willing to invest that much into the protection of your work, can you honestly say that you are serious about it? There have been plenty of times when I did not have the copyright fee immediately but the instant I got the money, I made the sacrifice and cut out something from my budget because I know that my ideas are priceless. And so are yours. So, treat them as valuables and get them the protection they deserve.

It is best to protect your work when it is in the final version that you will present to people, rather than doing so before it is complete. Any changes made to the registered version have to be re-registered for Copyright protection.

To Do

Write out the full execution of your pitch. If you are looking for a job, give details on what you want your compensation package to look like, what type of benefits you desire. For a television show or film, write down details of your story.

Already, some of you are feeling like this is too much work and you just want to get to the part where I tell you how to get the meeting. This is all a part of the process.

Remember the movie "The Karate Kid"? You may not understand why the steps are necessary individually but when combined as a whole, you will put yourself far ahead of those who try to sidestep the process.

Use the next page to make bullet points about your synopsis or summary of everything that happens - the major story points or the major deal points if you are job hunting.

Write out your breakdown:

What is the genre of your project? What is the job title you are seeking?

What is your logline? What is your career objective?

Who are the main characters? Are you casting them or do you already have talent attached? Either way, detail why each one is the right person to be involved. If you are job hunting, write your ideal job description.

How many episodes do you have? How many scenes are in the screenplay? What happens in each to move the story forward? If you are job hunting, write down the experience you have that will contribute to your job search.

Prepare your treatment/work and register it through the appropriate agency to establish your rights.

For Copyright Registration:

US Copyright Office www.copyright.gov

Use Form TX - For Literary Works (i.e. Books)

Use Form PA - For Performance Material (i.e. Screenplays)

Use Form VA - For Visual Content (i.e. Films)

Use Form SE - For Single Serials (i.e. Newspapers)

Use Form SR - For Sound Recordings (Note: If you are owner of the lyrics of a song as well as the music, this form will cover both.)

To Register Treatments, Stageplays, Lyrics Music and other Media Work:

WGA (Writer's Guild of America) Registry www.wgawregistry.org

Print out your receipts and write down your registration information and keep it in a safe place until your receive the official notification in the mail.

3. Research

Do you know whom you want to meet with when presenting a project? If you are seeking employment, who is the person you want to land as primary interviewer for a job opening? While that sounds like a basic question, many people are so eager to meet a person in the "industry" that they don't take the time to find out if it makes any sense at all to meet with them.

Do you know if something similar to your pitch is already in development or production?

Don't settle for just getting into a company. Be as specific as figuring exactly who you want to meet. Details such as those will get you closer to your goal.

Although I had no experience or training in writing, when I attended my first pitch session I was told by several executives that my pitch was the best they had heard that day. This included executives who had no interest in what I was pitching.

I think the main reason my pitch was so well received was because I had done tons of research long before I got up the nerve to even attend a Screenwriter's Conference.

It wasn't just one area of research that helped me. For at least three years, I "lived" with my characters before I put them down on paper. They were like friends in my head. I knew each of their histories and could anticipate what their next move might be.

I had spent much time developing my characters and the screenplay concept itself. But, as I wrote I had no movie studio or production company in mind, simply because I was writing the story that I feel needed to be told.

Honestly, when I wrote that screenplay at least 15 years ago, I never dreamed that I would let anyone else read it, let alone pitch it before studio executives and production companies.

And I had no idea that of ALL of the studios, production companies and agents that attended that year's American Screenwriter's Association conference that HBO would be the one to request a copy of my screenplay.

Someone reading this may have picked up this book simply because are curious about the process. Others may be further along in their careers and just need to know some best practices about pitching. Yet others want to be able to apply this information in venturing into a new career.

No matter your reason for reading this book, I strongly advise you to spend as much time as possible on the critical research process. It can make a difference in whether or not you get doors opened to you or have them remain closed.

In addition, you don't want to find yourself presented with an opportunity without be prepared to receive it. Because then, you are only relying on luck.

I recently met someone who convinced an Executive that she was such a huge fan of a major celebrity that she needed to meet him. She had no plan, but she knew that she wanted to meet the celeb and find a way to work with him.

Although the Executive did not know the personality, he reached out to his personal network of resources and sure enough, was directly introduced to the celebrity's manager. He then did an e-mail introduction to the young lady and she was invited to come to meet with a member of the celebrity's team the next time she was in LA.

What an amazing opportunity! However, about a month or so later, the young lady contacted me and told me that the celeb had relocated out of the country and so there was no chance that she would connect with him in LA, since she lives in NY.

Little did she know that the talent moving out of the country was not her biggest challenge, at least not in my opinion. Her main issue was that she had no pitch! If she got the meeting, her plan was to talk about the celebrity and why she would be an asset to his team. He already has a team.

My advice to her was simple: find out what he is lacking and see if you can fill that need. After we spoke, she realized that she needed to have something specific to communicate with the manager about, otherwise, she would risk jeopardizing a valuable relationship before it even got started.

Research before she made the connection would have put her in a different space than she was in at that time and could have garnered an opportunity for her.

If you are meeting with a production company, does your project fit within their body of work? What type of shows have they already produced? If your pitch is for television, what does your targeted network's programming slate look like? If you are shopping a comedic screenplay, has the production company produced only animation?

Do you know if something similar to your pitch is already in production? Keep in mind that you are not the only brain in the game. While the execution of your project may be unique unto you, other people may have been pitching similar ideas long beforehand and ended up in meetings while you were still fine-tuning your concept.

To determine if you are meeting with the appropriate production company or network, check out shows that are similar to yours. Visit www.imdb.com to determine the production company heading up the show and see if you can score a meeting with them.

While seeking talent for my radio show, I wanted to reach the creator of a major television series on ABC for an interview. I went to the IMDB website, got the information for the production company and was able to contact her assistant directly. Not only was I connected with the Press Rep, but I was also told to make sure I copied the assistant on all correspondence with the agent. Copying the assistant would help make sure my needs were met and that my request was filled in a timely manner.

If you want to find out what is currently being produced in your area, check out the Office of Film and Television. In New York the website is www.nyc.gov/html/film/

Read trade publications online such as The Hollywood Reporter, Deadline Hollywood, The Wrap and Cynopsis to keep abreast of new projects and be aware of industry trends and changes.

Variety online publishes a TV Pilot/Development Scorecard, which identifies by television network, show titles, studio, above the line staff (i.e. Executive Producers, Writers, Director), the logline and in some cases a status of projects in various stages of development. That's a great resource to determine if you are thinking along the lines of other content creators in your genre and an invaluable resource to get names of the key players at the companies you want to contact.

You should also research to make sure you are meeting with the right person. Just as you would not want a real estate attorney to review your recording contract or reality show treatment and regard them as a professional, neither should you share your ideas with just anyone in the industry who is willing to listen.

Here's a very valuable tip, in case you haven't already figured it out:

Each major company has an email protocol. For example at my Digital Media Agency, amass digital;

it is simply first name@amassdigital.com. If you want to contact an Executive directly, use the resources above to get the email address of anyone in the company. That will unlock the key to getting directly in touch with the person you want to contact.

However, BEWARE. Don't develop a bad reputation for spamming. Respect those who do not accept unsolicited pitches and never, ever send a person you want to develop a long-term business relationship an email where they are being blind copied with hundreds of others. They know.

Even worse, don't send a mass email with every email address exposed. I've been the victim of being added to multiple lists that I never signed up for. I can always trace it back to an email where someone copied myself and 100 other people without protecting the privacy of my email address.

I once used that tip to get in touch with the head of a utility company that was consistently exhibiting horrible customer service. No one questioned how I got the email of their top executive. I laid out my case, aligning facts with dates and my desired outcome. I was contacted, given an actual appointment of my choosing (instead of a four hour window) and the cell phone number of an assistant who not only was willing to take my call if the technician did not show up on time, but took the time to call me while he was there to ensure things were running smoothly.

Another way to reach professionals is on LinkedIn. Make sure you enter your complete profile and customize it with pictures, links, etc. You may already know someone connected to the people you want to meet who might be willing to do an introduction. I've even received job offers, speaking engagements and pitches directly from my LinkedIn page.

No matter what you are pitching, look at similar things that have been successfully pitched. If there's a television show in the same genre as yours, why not pitch it to the Production Company that produced the show? If there's a film that you like, try to get a copy of the screenplay. There are a few websites such as IMSDb and The Daily Script that have screenplays available for download. And if you ever wanted to see the pilot script for your favorite television show, more than likely you can find it online at GoodInARoom.com

You are one step closer to being ready to set up your pitch meeting!

To Do

List at least five production companies that you want to hear your pitch. If you are job hunting, list five companies you'd most like to meet. Include the name of the appropriate person and research the best way to get in touch with them. Enter their contact information in the next few pages for quick reference.

Company 1

Company Name and Address:

Contact Name:

Contact Phone Number:

Contact Email Address:

Who do you know that may be willing to facilitate an introduction?

Company 2

Company Name and Address:

Contact Name:

Contact Phone Number:

Contact Email Address:

Who do you know that may be willing to facilitate an introduction?

Company 3

Company Name and Address:

Contact Name:

Contact Phone Number:

Contact Email Address:

Who do you know that may be willing to facilitate an introduction?

Company 4

Company Name and Address:

Contact Name:

Contact Phone Number:

Contact Email Address:

Who do you know that may be willing to facilitate an introduction?

Company 5

Company Name and Address:

Contact Name:

Contact Phone Number:

Contact Email Address:

Who do you know that may be willing to facilitate an introduction?

If you are not already on LinkedIn, sign up for an account. It's a powerful tool to get you connected to people you want to know, while showcasing what you have to offer at the same time.

Find the five people you have listed above and see if they are on LinkedIn. Are you remotely connected to them? If so, note the person you are connected to on LinkedIn that may be able to make an introduction.

Whether you are connected or not, the next chapter will help you tap into the power of networking and bring you closer to securing the meeting you want.

4. Network

One of the most effective ways to ensure that you are meeting with the best person to move your career forward is to network.

Before we discuss what networking is and a few ways to be successful in that regard, I feel it's necessary to guide you into the correct networking mindset. This is by far where many people feel defeated before they get started and where they close doors before they even have the chance to open for them.

Networking Isn't Spam

As a creative on of the thing that stops me from helping people get closer to their dreams in the entertainment industry is spam.

Social media is a networking TOOL. But, it's not networking. I have received countless links on Twitter. I've altered my Facebook settings to that no one can post without my permission. Some people seem to think the best way to "network" is to spend several hours each day, sending their link and a generic phrase such as "show some support" or "check this out" to random people on Twitter. That is not networking.

In fact, when I receive a tweet from someone whom I've never interacted with before, the first thing I do is check his or her timeline. If I see that they have sent the same tweet, merely copy and pasting to anyone and everyone, I instantly block them. Why?

Because I believe in protecting my energy and I believe my timeline, my words and the energy surrounding them are valuable. It's not that deep for some people. It is for me.

On a few occasions, I have replied to the person that is spamming and they become angry, because they don't see it as spam. It's spam. Especially if you don't even know the person you are addressing. There is a proper way to approach people on social media. In fact, when I was writing an article about advice that people in entertainment would give to their younger selves, I reached out to a former host of The View and asked if I could get her response to a question for the article. She sent me a direct message telling me to ask the question. I got the quote for my article.

Networking Isn't a Hook-Up

What would be more valuable to you? A one time "hook-up" or tools that put you on the path to success? It's like feeding a hungry person a fish sandwich versus teaching them to fish. One is temporary and the other is the gift of knowledge they will benefit from eternally.

There are times when I have been asked to make an introduction to someone of influence and I have not. The most prevalent reason is because the person isn't ready for the intro. A networking introduction should never be for the purpose of just getting to know one another without any thought of how the relationship can be mutually beneficial.

By the same token, you should manage your expectations when you are introduced to someone of influence.

Your Man's and 'Em

My friends laugh at me every time I use this phrase. Beware of "your man's and 'em". Who are they? They are the people in your life who are able to develop relationships with people of influence but are nothing more than outsiders with an insider's view. They are people who want to introduce you to someone for a "finder's fee". They seek to exploit their relationships with others simply for financial gain.

You may see them with pictures of celebs posted all over social media and they have amazing stories to tell but they offer no real value or insight into ways to advance your career. Just look at where they are standing. Don't misconstrue your interactions with them as networking.

What is Help?

I once helped someone develop their brand and their strategy. We no longer speak because he feels as if I didn't want to 'help' him.

His sole desire was to make money traveling. At least that was his initial objective as expressed to me. I gave him information on how to pitch himself to hotels and restaurants and suggested that he start with a travel blog so that people could associate a value with him coming in to review their venue.

Within a short period of time he secured a complimentary hotel stay and was invited to do a taste testing of the entire menu at a new restaurant. He continued to follow the advice I gave him while growing his presence online.

He then decided that he wanted to sell t-shirts. Here's the first time it got tricky. He's not a designer. He wanted to sell the t-shirts to build brand awareness. As I write this book I am preparing for a Trade Show and I will be giving away t-shirts. I know where my gifts and talents lie and while I can sew, I am no clothing designer. They are giveaway promotional items.

After all that I shared with him, he got angry because his family and friends were not showing support by purchasing his $50 t-shirts. No, that's not a typo. $50. When he expressed the concern I told him that buying the t-shirts wouldn't help him. Sure, it might put money in his pocket, but his friends and family were not in his demo. He wanted to reach upscale celebrities. Then he decided to try to get celebrities to wear his t-shirts. Guess who he wanted a hook-up from in the name of 'help'.

The next time it got sticky spelled the end of the relationship. He had a major opportunity to secure a sponsorship with a Jet company. I gave recommendations on what should be included in the pitch and his response was to email it to me so I could mark it up for him after I told him that I didn't have time to meet his deadline.

As he told me he hit the send button, I said simply "I got it and I deleted it."

When you are seeking help and someone is kind enough to offer it, graciously accept what is offered to you. To insist that they do more than they are willing or capable of is to be self-centered and unappreciative of their efforts on your behalf.

In another instance, one of my Twitter followers asked me to write for his blog. For free. When I told him that I would have to see his blog to make sure that it was a fit with my branding, he first told me that he thought I wanted to help him. Then he told me that he had not yet started his blog.

Needless to say, I'm a lot more careful about the inquiries I entertain since then.

Be clear: NO ONE IS OBLIGATED TO HELP YOU. The greatest help anyone can ever give you is information that sets you on the road you need to travel.

Remember the Wizard of Oz? What was the most valuable piece of information that each character in the movie gave to Dorothy? And then what was the most valuable information that she gave to the Scarecrow, the Tin Man and the Lion? It was where they needed to go and how to get there. There would not have been much of a story without us seeing the journey of each character on the road to meeting the Powerful Oz. The Good Witch Glenda could have flown Dorothy to the Land of Oz on her magic broomstick at any given moment. But, what would have been the value in that?

The same applies to our path to success. I was told by the very individual that I helped find a way to pursue his passion that because I have certain gifts and talents and did not use them to benefit him the way he saw fit, God won't bless me. That's not true. I am not the savior of the world and I can't help everyone. However, my way of helping is by writing books that can help anyone on their journey. In fact, if you need inspiration on your journey, be sure to check out my Inspiration book series: "Dear God: Passionate Prayers in 140 Characters or Less" at www.DearGodBook.com

Appreciate the journey and don't interfere with your success by taking shortcuts or negating the help that others offer to you.

Now, on to Networking.

Grow Your Net Worth with Your Network

With advances in social media, networking no longer has to be limited to in person events. At the least, start a Twitter or Facebook account. If you are job hunting, I can't emphasize how important it is that you join LinkedIn. Once you join those social media sites, interact with and follow people who interests similar to yours. You never know which person holds the key to the door you are trying to enter.

Many people think that social media is nothing more than people talking about what they ate and how often they brushed their teeth. There may be people who discuss those things on social media, but I don't know any of them.

In fact, I got a very high paying gig in television from a woman who followed me on Twitter for two years before approaching me when the right opportunity presented itself.

She watched what I wrote about, how I wrote it and whom I interacted with. In fact, she started following me because a celebrity with more than 1 million followers suggested that his audience should follow me.

One night after "live tweeting" an episode of a television show which featured a troubled rapper whom I had developed and pitched a series about, she followed the link in my Twitter bio and contacted me via my website.

Imagine my surprise when I received an email asking if I was interested in writing for a television show soon to be in production! She noticed that I had no writing credits in television but felt that based on what she had been reading on my timeline for TWO YEARS that I was a perfect fit for the show she was Executive Producing.

One of the best networking mindsets is to seek people who would mutually benefit from your interaction. While there are some people who are willing to help, you will attract more positivity to your initiative if you are seeking to fill a need, rather than have your chief motive be that of getting those of your own met.

One of the best ways to increase your net worth within your network is to understand the principle of what I refer to as the "value proposition."

I don't believe that you should ever do anything for free. But, what is the value of free? When I started as a writer, I need to get credit in magazines and online websites so that I could have a portfolio of writing samples. So I wrote for free. But what was the value proposition of "free?"

I need the recognition. The websites needed quality content. It was a balanced win-win, with each of our needs being met, without money exchanging hands.

Attend conferences, workshops and share your dreams with people around you. I have met influential people in the airport, on a train, bus, via e-mail, and at the doctor's office. Realize that each person you meet represents a chance to get you one step closer to the person you want to meet.

Get to know those who have done or are doing what it is you desire to do. If you want to get your show on the air, do you know anyone who has ever worked in television? If you have a screenplay that you want to see on the big screen, do you know any friends or family involved in acting?

Those questions are important for more than just an introduction to the person. Don't be misled by well-meaning friends and family who love your idea out of loyalty to you. Get to know people who can give you an honest opinion about your work and advise you about the path you are taking.

Who was I? I had no college degree, no experience and this was my first screenplay. I never took a writing course. I learned about script formatting online and had purchased the industry standard software.

While well intentioned family and friends will rally their "support" of your project, trust me, there's nothing more affirming than having someone who is an expert in your field tell you that you are on the right track.

I wrote my first screenplay more than 10 years ago. I went to a Screenwriter's Conference and pitched, although I had never done it before.

When I was told that my pitch was "the best of the day" by several of the Executives in attendance, and a major movie studio requested my screenplay, my insecurity got the best of me.

Who was I? I had no college degree, no experience and this was my first screenplay. I never took a writing course. I learned about script formatting online and had purchased the industry standard software. Oh, I was prepared for my pitch. I had an opportunity. But, what I needed most was a network.

I needed people around me, who were doing what I was doing to give me the confidence to move forward, without falling flat on my face. I needed people who understood my challenges in being a mom, having a family and choosing between a job that paid the bills and following my passion. I needed to speak with someone who had experienced what I was feeling and could guide me through what to expect.

Build your network. Make sure you find cheerleaders - people who are excited about you and the projects you are intending to pitch.

No matter how prepared you are, when the opportunity comes along, your network will keep you focused, grounded and guide you through the process.

Your network will also expand your opportunities. I attended a conference in New York two years ago and took the initiative to meet each of the speakers on a panel that interested me most.

I developed relationships with several of the people on the panel and as a result, a few months later, I was tapped to speak at a music industry conference in Orlando. In addition, I landed two clients as a result of my attendance at that conference.

As if that weren't enough, I began mentoring a young lady who introduced me to the Black Public Relations Society of New York. I became active with that organization and now sit on the Board of Directors.

I think that workshop cost me $60. But the benefit I derived from doing more than just showing up and taking the initiative to develop and maintain relationships netted me more than 100 times my initial investment. Talk about a winning value proposition!

To Do

Find a group of people in your area who are already doing what you aspire to do. If you have a friend who is in the line of work you want to be in, go meet up with them. If you can't find a social group, attend a class, seminar or workshop and stay in touch with at least 3 people you meet in the class.

This will be an ongoing exercise, but develop the relationship so that you can have someone to pitch to. They can help you with the next step as well.

5. Practice

The next thing you need to know before you pitch seems simple, but it makes it easier if you have followed all of the steps above.

No matter how much work you have done on your pitch up until now, you need to practice.

Try to develop a 30, 60 and 90 second version of your pitch. If you cannot describe your concept in three sentences or whittle it down to one paragraph, you haven't fully defined it. These are referred to as "elevator" pitches.

I once took advantage of being alone in an elevator with the President of MTV by pitching a show to him, based on information he had shared with the company at an offsite meeting the day before. The pitch was relevant and short. By the end of the ride, he told me to contact the head of Development and tell him that HE had sent me.

As often as I had practiced my pitch, the only reason I was able to explain it passionately and intelligently with confidence is because I KNEW what I was talking about. I KNEW that it was relevant to what the network was looking for. In addition, I knew I had limited time and was done with my pitch before he got off the elevator.

Before practicing with those who aspire to be your competition, recite your pitch aloud to yourself in the mirror. While it might sound crazy, see if you can get your idea across completely without a verbal stumble. I never realized how frequently the word "um" appeared in my vocabulary until I started playing back the audio of my radio show.

Now that you have pulled it all together and are ready to set up the big meeting, reach out to the people you networked with and ask if you can practice your pitch with them.

Make sure the person you choose to practice your pitch with will be totally honest and will ask questions that will lead you to a stronger pitch.

For those of you who are saying you are not a good networker and you don't know anyone remotely interested in hearing your pitch, check out the Meetup website. They have a host of groups geared towards your specific interests all across the country.

To Do

Write out your pitch. Writing out your pitch is important because it forces you to be clear and concise. Measure your level of excitement as you explain your project. Try three different pitches and see which one you are more comfortable with.

Pitch 1:

Pitch 2:

Pitch 3:

Time your 30, 60 and 90 second pitches by recording yourself on your cell phone. Make sure you cover the who, what, where and when of your project. Include the why only if it doesn't give away the entire premise.

Use the space below to make notes on your timing and decide which part of your pitch you can trim or what information you can add if you are falling short.

Share your pitch with your family or a close friend, just so that you can get comfortable with idea of sharing your concept. This can be the hardest part.

There have been times when I've had ideas that I thought people would laugh at or just would not "get". I am blessed to have a friend who is willing to read everything that I write and several other friends that I can share pitches with.

Networking will afford you those opportunities and enable you to reciprocate when they need an ear as well.

Once you are comfortable with pitching to your family, reach out to someone you have met recently by networking. Listen to their criticism and adjust accordingly.

5 THINGS NEVER TO SAY OR DO IN A PITCH

Now that you have spent a considerable amount of time refining your pitch, identifying who you are going to present it to and practicing, let's prepare you for the actual pitch day.

There are plenty of things that you should never do or say if you want all of your preparation to matter when you have the opportunity to pitch.

What follows are five things that I have heard or seen happen either when taking pitches or hearing back from others on how their meeting went.

I cringed as I knew that some of their actions would mean that their first meeting would probably be their last.

In this case, it's not simply a matter of how you say what you say, but it is important to know what to say and not to say as well as what to do and not to do.

Let's look at a list of "don'ts".

1. "It's a No-Brainer!"

Everyone knows that you think your idea is the greatest. Your opinion should only fuel your passion about the project and not a superiority complex.

Respect the experience of the person with whom you are meeting. To infer that your concept is so brilliant and that someone MUST work with you implies that they are an idiot and you know their job better than they do.

In your brain, it might be an obvious fit for the network or production company you are pitching to. But, their brain is what matter most.

The last thing you want to do is shoot yourself in the foot with your demeanor. Do not alienate the chance to build a relationship with someone simply because your approach is condescending.

While it seems like a common sense thing, you would be surprised at how many times people approach an interview or pitch in this manner.

I am not saying that you should lack confidence. Again, be fueled by passion for your project or during your job interview. However, your idea of a "win-win" situation may not be appealing to the person you are presenting to.

Often the person you are meeting with will have to pitch you or your idea to other people. It would be in your best interests to present yourself in a manner that would give them a reason to choose you to pitch up the ladder instead of the other people who they met with before you and will meet with after you.

Keep in mind that while the meeting may not lead to a closed deal, it can be the start of a relationship that can open many doors for you and ultimately lead to your goal. To risk it all by insulting the person potentially holding the key to your future would not be smart at all.

While I was working at MTV, I had someone pitch me a DJ competition show. The pitch sounded familiar, as I had pitched a similar show to the network. In fact, my person in Development told me that about 7 other people had pitched a similar show as well.

Instead of accepting my response telling them that I knew there would be no interest, the person became indignant and remarked to me that people didn't believe in another show that was on the network when it was first pitched but that a Celebrity Judge attached to the show had fought to get it on the air.

I couldn't confirm or deny her account because it wasn't a show that I worked on. However, based on the fact that she felt entitled in some way that I should pitch her show just because she thought it was a good idea was enough for me to cancel out the possibility of ever working with her.

Remember that the person you are pitching to is in the position of authority for a reason. You want to speak with them because of their knowledge and their ability to get things done. Don't belittle them and perhaps jeopardize a chance for you to develop a long-term beneficial relationship. When you approach someone who is a subject matter expert, do not discount their expertise simply because you don't like what they say about your project.

2. "I know it's never been done before."

I cannot count the number of times I have heard those words uttered by people who are determined to believe that their idea works simply because of it's "originality".

Networks, production companies, and even employers are not looking for something that's never "been done" before. When I first started pitching, I asked a development executive what I should most keep in mind as I come up with ideas for shows. She told me that no matter the network I pitched to, make sure that I was an avid viewer of their content. Knowing this will help to make sure that my idea was similar to what they were airing, yet nothing like it and more importantly would fit their demo.

In addition she told me that networks want more of the same, except expressed differently. It is no accident that there are so many singing competition shows, reality shows featuring famous exes, cooking shows and crime dramas. The people who pitched those shows started with a basic premise and made it work for the network they were interested in working with.

How often is groundbreaking content developed? How many times have you seen a groundbreaking film? It happens, but it is not a daily occurrence.

The strength of your pitch should lie in your concept and not in the fact that it has never "been done" before. There are probably valid reasons why it hasn't been done and uniqueness alone is not enough to bring people on board with you.

Furthermore, your project may not be an appropriate fit. Attempting to force your idea to fit within the parameters of the network is a clear indication that you have not done the research and that your creative is not strong enough as it needs to be.

The fact that it's never "been done" before should not weigh heavily into the justification of the validity of your project.

3. NEVER Embellish

While this may not be your first pitch; it may be your fifth pitch for the same show. If someone in a previous meeting indicated any interest, don't overstate the truth. Someone who was appearing as talent on a major cable network show once approached me to ask if I would be a producer on a show the network was giving to them. She told me they had closed a deal and she would begin casting soon for her sizzle reel. But, then I found out she was paying for to shoot her own pilot. The network wasn't paying for the pilot, which meant to me that there was no show.

Two days later, I ran into the executive producer of the show she was appearing on and congratulated him on the success of the "new show". As I suspected, he quickly told me that there was no "show". He thought the show was a good idea. However, he felt it would be difficult to cast and that if they could overcome that hurdle, then they MIGHT do a deal.

There's this old school myth in the entertainment industry that you can create a "bidding war". There is no fire, where there's no flame. Deceptively implying that other networks, production companies or talent are attached to your project will not increase your chances of getting your project made.

Be honest about your previous meetings. If someone is interested in working with you, this may not be the project that gets the deal closed. A sure fire way to make sure that you don't get considered at all is to lie. The industry is too small for your claims not to be verified.

In any event, never embellish. If your cousin is the janitor at a cable network and likes your pitch, do not refer to him as a representative of the company.

Just because a celebrity on twitter retweeted a sentence from your story line, does not mean they co-signed it.

During my time at Iconic TV, I was once in a meeting and noticed that a young lady who looked vaguely familiar was sitting in the lobby area. She sat there throughout most of my meeting, but left just before I was done.

I asked the receptionist who the young lady was and learned, ironically enough, she had asked to speak with me. Apparently we had met briefly at a networking event and I gave her my business card.

It was weird to me that someone would show up to my office unannounced, however, the receptionist gave me her phone number and I called the young lady.

She told me that she had sent me a pitch over a month ago and that I never replied. The truth was that she had tried to set up several meetings with me, despite me wanting to follow up with a simple phone call.

I had responded to her, in fact, to tell her that the idea she was pitching was similar to something we were already developing for one of our YouTube channels. She replied to that email asking me for a meeting with one of co-owners of the company.

I believe that not every ringing phone needs to be answered, nor does every e-mail require a response. Her asking for the meeting was not appropriate and quite presumptive, so replying to her email was not on my list of priorities.

When I asked her why she chose to randomly drop by my office, she said she was in the area. She then continued the call by name-dropping. She told me that she had pitched her show idea to the Chief Creative Officer of the company and he was interested in her pitch. I told her since that was the case; she needed to follow up with him directly.

Of course, as soon as I got off the phone with her, I walked into his office. She had no way of knowing that I landed my job at the company as a direct result of being a Producer for a show on Vh1 that was Executive Produced by that Executive and his production company in addition to our work together previously.

After doing a quick search of his e-mail he realized that someone else, not her, had pitched the idea to him, which he had already passed on.

That scenario had crazy written all over it. However, let it be a cautionary tale of why you should never name drop or embellish the truth in anything related to your project or prospective employment.

4. NEVER alter your concept "on the fly"

The inspiration for this book came when I conducted a workshop as a presentation before company interns. Not altering "on the fly" was the only point that an Emmy-winning owner of a very successful television production and former head of development at a major network disagreed with. Once I explained in depth; he got the point.

There are times that you are in a meeting and the person you are presenting to likes the idea but needs something else. It is not always in your best interests to alter your concept just to appease the person you are meeting with.

For example, the elevator pitch I gave to the President of MTV led to many conversations with people in the development department. I did have a Grammy Award winning, Multi-Platinum Music Artist attached to the show and it was a plus that he only wanted to be involved if he could Executive Produce. However, the network decided that the key element of my pitch, which is what stirred the interest of the talent, was something they felt their audience would not be interested in.

The only reason the celeb was interested was because there was a charity component. Months later after many e-mails and conference calls, I was told they wanted the show but not with the charitable undertones.

I didn't even need to go back to the celebrity or lead the network on. They didn't want the charity component, so that was the end of our discussion. I got a call a few months later from the network about the show. Only the name had been changed to the "Insert Talent Name" show. They were very interested in working with the talent to develop a new show.

I did not want to continue talks just for the sake of trying to convince the network to do the show. The show is what it is, with or without that particular talent attachment. The network clearly wanted the talent more than the show. And the only way the talent would do the show was diametrically opposed to what the network wanted.

They are times when what the network wants is feasible within the parameters of your creative. While you should always be open to work with the network or production company to change your concept (because they will), you should allow them to steer the conversation and see if it is still makes sense for you to pursue the project.

Never be so desperate for an opportunity that you commit to something that you are not capable of doing or handling, just because you want to close a deal.

5. NEVER impose on anyone's time

Respect the time of the person with whom you are meeting. Don't put yourself on the "never take a call or meeting" list. Your first impression is important and can result in this being your first meeting and maybe your last.

If there is no interest in your idea, graciously accept that. Ask politely when would be a good time to share other ideas. There might be an opportunity for you to do so, but it may not be in the same meeting.

Always be prepared to pitch, but do not impose your agenda upon the person with whom you are meeting. Dumping your entire creative brain into their lap when they were specifically interested in one idea is not the right approach.

The same applies if you are asked to submit a screenplay. Pay attention to what is being requested. If the meeting requires a treatment or synopsis, send exactly what is needed. Don't ever send a full script without getting permission to do so.

I once did a consultation with someone who asked me to critique a pitch they developed for a potentially major opportunity. As we reached the end of our 15-minute allocated time, the person asked if I would mind reviewing their written materials. When I told them that I did not have time, their response was "well, I e-mailed it to you just in case you have some free time later."

Never assume that any person is willing to spend more than the allotted time with you. If they are interested and time permits, they will ask you to stay or ask that you set up another meeting with them. In my book "Opening Doors: Getting Connected," I tell the story of meeting a major music industry executive after jokingly offering to pay him as a token of my appreciation for 15 minutes of his time. After he laughed, we set a meeting and I was there for more than an hour.

Don't ever seek to impose your timeframe upon other people. It reeks of desperation and will alienate you from potentially rewarding relationships and opportunities.

I get many requests to meet with people inside the office as well as outside. Those I give a quicker yes to are those who respect my time. When first meeting someone, 15 minutes is appropriate.

Pay attention to verbal or physical clues that may be telling you that you need to end the meeting. It could mean the difference between getting another chance or not.

5 THINGS YOU SHOULD ALWAYS DO IN A PITCH

Now that you've gotten the things that you shouldn't say or do out of the way, let's look at some of the things that you should always do in a pitch.

Keep in mind that this is not intended as an exhaustive list, however these are things that will get you noticed and improve your changes of getting back into the room again.

When I first printed this information as a short form e-book several years ago, I sent a free copy to someone who had reached out to me for help on social media.

After reading a shortened version of this book, which I got an email from the young man who told me in colorful words that he was not going to kiss anyone's bottom in order to become successful.

That was three years ago. He's still on Social Media spamming people links to try to get them to listen to his music. This is work. But, it's worth it.

1. Introduce Yourself

Many people shortchange themselves in the most basic step of the meeting that could be the launching pad for a successful career.

More importantly than merely stating your name, you should remind the person of the purpose of your meeting and give them some background information on why you are presenting this particular pitch. Be certain to mention any relevant experience to the subject matter because it could immediately establish some credibility.

For example, if you are pitching a weight-loss show or film about a person who is bi-polar, quickly establish your previous work in the health care field, your battle with weight loss or anything that would express why you are passionate about this project. Companies have the option to do business and spend money with any number of people. Explain to them why it should be you.

If you discover in your research that you and the person you are meeting attended the same school, came from the same state or have anything else in common, establish that before starting your pitch. Mention whom you may know in common, especially if you have a relationship with someone who knows them.

Familiarity can set the tone for the meeting and could provide a reason to develop the relationship further.

To Do

Put together a bio that lists all of your experience and knowledge of the subject matter pertaining to your pitch.

The first time I was interviewed on a radio show, I listened as the host introduced me to the audience. I was so blown away by her detailing of my work and accomplishments that the first thing I said was "Who is SHE? I want to be that person you just introduced."

I've found that other people often see us much bigger than we see ourselves. Ask your friends and colleagues who are aware of your experiences in your field of interest to describe what you do and list your major accomplishments. Each time I do this, I am amazed at how much I forget about myself. Use this space to write their observations about you and then integrate their comments into your bio and determine which highlights pertain to your pitch meeting.

2. Be Gracious

Thank the person for taking the time to meet with you at the beginning and end of the meeting. Whether you agree with them or not, let them know you appreciate their thoughts and any advice they offered.

Even if the idea is not a match, don't knock the chance of anything potential in the future. Don't develop a sour disposition if you are not received as well as you'd like to be.

I went to an interview once that was cancelled five minutes after it started because of a last minute company priority. Although I was crushed internally and tempted to believe that what I was saying did not hold the interest of the person, I did not let it show. I graciously thanked them for their time, with no sign of my disappointment.

As I traveled home, I wondered what the appropriate follow-up would be. I received an e-mail saying the crisis was diverted along with an apology for the cancellation. The interview was rescheduled, and I ended up getting the job.

On my first day, I was told that the reason I was hired was because I did not take the cancellation personally. My professionalism showed through at a time when it may not have for others.

Pay attention to verbal and physical cues. Know when to stop speaking and know when they are asking for more information. Determine when to move on from one point if it's not working or to shift gears as necessary.

Another example of how being gracious pays off is what happened when I sent a thank you note to a former President of MTV who I feel greatly influenced my career.

Once she left the network, I had no way to contact her except through Facebook. I sent a brief note, letting her know that her mission to help us to use the "M" to define our values actually helped me focus on my purpose.

Imagine my surprise just earlier this year, when I ran into her at the NAACP Image Awards. When I mentioned my name, she said, "You're a writer, aren't you?" That meant the world to me, because it meant she had in some way been following my trajectory and noticed that I am not just working in television.

In my book "Opening Doors: Getting Connected", which about developing relationships within the entertainment industry and beyond, I devote an entire chapter to the importance of saying thank you and meaning it because it's an area that is often overlooked. Keep in mind that everyone you meet, whether for a pitch or a job interview, already has a job. They made a decision to set aside time to meet with you. Show some appreciation, no matter how the meeting ends.

3. Be Concise

I once attended a screenwriting conference where each person we presented to would only receive one pitch in the five-minute time slot we were allocated. When you have your elevator pitch broken down to 90 seconds, and the logline succinctly conveys what your concept is, five minutes is a lot of time.

People can often tell if they are interested shortly after you begin to speak. When I was in the music industry, I sat in offices with A&R people who would listen to the first few bars or only 30 to 60 seconds of a song before hitting the stop or fast forward button.

I have also been in the scenario of starting my pitch and being abruptly told that they had heard the same type of show pitched to them several times.

There was no need for a lengthy discussion; however, I was pleasantly surprised when I was asked if I had anything else to pitch. I later found out from a development person that she thought I had great pitch formats. Now a personal friend of mine, she admitted that she loved to hear my pitches because they were concise and gave her a good idea of whether or not she was interested.

When people realize that you are not wasting their time, they are willing to spend more of it with you.

Being concise gives the listener a chance to pass and is potentially an opportunity for you to share more of your ideas.

4. Relax

Sweaty palms and a nervous twitch tend to be distracting.

Enjoy the moment – this is your time to shine. No matter what happens, you were invited to the meeting for a reason. Show your host that you appreciate both their time and interest.

I can't tell you how to calm your nerves on the spot. No matter how many times I pitch, my heart is in my throat each time. Why? Because we only pitch what we are passionate about. Each time we are laying our hopes, dreams and desires out in the open for someone to dissect. That's a huge risk to take. But, don't shrink back. Be brave.

I can tell you that if you come prepared and follow the steps in 5 Things to DO BEFORE a Pitch, your level of stress will decrease greatly. Knowing what and how to present is more than half of the battle.

Realize that there is a process, and it never happens that you walk out of the door with a contract in hand.

Set very basic, realistic expectations for the meeting and don't panic if you don't get the desired result.

Take the time to breathe and give the required focus and attention to each topic. There are no wrong answers. You are presenting your idea. If you are pitching to the right person at the right company, you may not get a deal, but it will not be a waste of their time or yours.

5. Ask About Follow-Up

We've all been there. Anxiously waiting for a response with questions circling in our head and spiraling out of control. We check our email constantly, as if there's suddenly something wrong because we haven't received a response within a few days.

You can save yourself, your friends, and family unnecessary angst by asking a simple question.

"What happens next?"

Depending on how your meeting went, your idea may be pitched at a development meeting, discussed with other people or more. If there is interest, there will be forward movement.

Acquainting yourself with the next step in the process will help you to set realistic expectations and alleviate any lingering insecurity.

When I was job hunting, I would always close my interview with "just one more question." Each time, I would ask "So when do you want me to start?" I am sure that some people thought I was a bit presumptive, however, each time I asked, I got a realistic timeline of not only when I could expect to hear whether or not I got the job, but also an indication of the actual start date for the position, whether it was mine or not.

There's nothing wrong with asking when it would be appropriate for you to follow up. Always ask for a business card of the person you met with and if necessary, ask them to explain their decision making process and where you currently fit into that timeline.

It will save you many sleepless nights and feelings of rejection that are nothing more than someone taking the time to allow a necessary process to run its course.

5 THINGS TO DO AFTER A PITCH

Congratulations! You can now breathe a sigh of relief because your pitch meeting is over. Now, another level of anxiety sets in as you wonder what you should do next.

Let's start off with one of the most important things you need to do immediately after the pitch.

1. Follow Up

The last thing you should have done prior to leaving your meeting is to find out the appropriate follow-up method.

Following up actually falls into two categories. One should be done immediately after the meeting and the other should be done later.

Give Thanks

There are few things that are more underrated than a simple "thank you". In order to stand out from your competition, you want to make a lasting, memorable impression upon the people you meet. After all, you've invested a lot of time and effort in getting that appointment.

When I was a senior in High School, I won the Carol S. Schirmer award for excellence in Secretarial Skills. I had never even heard of the award and had no idea I won until the pre-graduation ceremony. I was awarded a certificate and a check for $50.

The first thing I did was ask who this woman was and how I could contact her. I found out that Mrs. Schirmer was an alma mater of my High School who was working at the Board of Education.

I went to the store and purchased a thank you card and handwrote a message to her thanking her for the award and her generosity, with no expectation of receiving a response.

Less than two weeks later, I got an envelope from the Board of Education. Mrs. Schirmer sent a thank you letter in reply to my thank you note telling me that not one of the previous recipients of the award had bothered to thank her.

She included a second check for $50.

Sadly, we live in a thankless world filled with people who have an air of entitlement. When you meet with someone and send them a genuine note of thanks, it stands out and is appreciated.

I would suggest that immediately following your meeting; you send an e-mail with a thank you and confirm the follow up method. For example, if you are told that you could expect a response the next week you could write:

"Thank you for taking the time to meet with me about (mention the project name). I enjoyed our conversation and look forward to hearing from you next week."

Status Update

You've sent your thank you note and it's been two whole weeks. All you hear is the sound of crickets. What's wrong?

As long as you remembered to get the follow up process from the person you were meeting with, this phase does not have to reduce you to tearful, sleepless and agita filled nights.

If you were told to call or email, follow that process within the specified timeframe and method the person indicated.

If you are told that you would receive a call within a few days or so and it does not happen, wait at least a week. It might seem like the longest week of your life, but you must remember that you are not dealing with people who are twirling their thumbs with nothing to do.

Don't automatically assume that a lack of response indicates a lack of interest. Many companies have processes and often the person you are meeting with will need to meet with someone else to pitch your pitch to them. If any person in that process gets sick, is out on vacation or a major project comes into play, it could result in a delayed response. Any number of factors could be the reason you have not yet heard back. The only way you will know for sure is with appropriate follow-up.

Should you receive another offer, or someone else expresses significant interest in your project, there's nothing wrong with sending a follow up note with the subject matter "Update re: (your project)".

I once interviewed for a job in January and while I got it, it took a significant amount of follow up. I finally started in April.

2. Heed Advice You Received

In the course of your meeting, you may be given ways to improve or change your concept that would make it more appealing to the network. If there's potential interest, you will be given the chance to make some changes to the execution of your concept prior to being called in for another meeting.

Don't walk out of the meeting feeling defeated as if you have "haters". Appreciate the advice given and apply it.

I once pitched two screenplays to an executive who told me that there was not a fit at that time for my work but for me to stay in touch with him because he would like to work with me in the future. Although it was a no, that opened the door for me to follow up with him about the next opportunity.

If it is decided that your idea is not fully developed or that the talent you have attached is not the right fit for the camera, accept the advice of a professional. It could be that you need to go back and research another place to pitch or it could mean that you need to do more work on your project.

No matter what you are told, don't give up.

You may have heard of Kentucky Fried Chicken, but did you know that many considered Colonel Sanders a failure until he finally sold his recipe for fried chicken? Not only was he 65 years old but he had also presented that recipe more than 1,000

times before he got started on the road to making it
a household name.

3. Re-Evaluate

After each pitch meeting or interview, assess what happened. Stick to the facts and leave out your personal feelings.

How did your meeting go? What could you have done better? What did you learn that you could apply to your next meeting? What research can you do to add to the value of your concept? Is there anything that you would have done differently?

Speak to those you practiced your pitch with and tell them how your meeting went. Ask for their input and be open to their advice.

4. Develop The Relationship

The end of the meeting does not have to signal the end of the relationship.

Follow up as previously discussed and seek ways to continue the communication far beyond your pitch.

Development executives often speak at conferences or are members of media organizations. If you recognize a name on the roster of the next workshop or networking event you attend, drop a quick note and let them know you plan to attend as well. Once you get to the event, make sure to go up to the person you met with and remind them of your meeting – whether it went well or not.

I was surprised when I attended a function and someone that I had previously pitched to was on the panel. I was even more delighted when he remembered me. During our conversation, he asked my thoughts on their contribution to the panel. We developed a relationship and as a result, I eventually worked on one of his television shows.

When appropriate, ask the person you met if you could take them for coffee to discuss a few ideas with them. When you read that they have a new show premiering, watch the show and drop a note letting them know how happy you are for them.

Everything else mentioned in this book would be to no avail if you put in all of the hard work of following the steps and don't continue the relationship. You will soon learn that the entertainment industry is small and if people like you, they will introduce you to other people who will benefit your career. In addition because the industry is so small, it doesn't hurt to have multiple people who know each other saying good things about you.

A lot of the work in television is on a freelance basis and is given to people who the production staff has already developed relationships with. If you want to have a thriving career in entertainment, building relationships is key.

5. Know What Matters

I have had a few of the same conversations with friends lately focused on our accomplishments compared to our peers.

You will see people who are less talented than you, seemingly less connected than you and who have been working for less time than you who seem to advance overnight with nominal effort. Don't pay attention to them.

I didn't write my first screenplay until I was in my 30's. I started my career in television while I was in my 40's. I didn't publish my first print edition of a book until I turned 50. Does that negate all of the years of experience I have in other fields such as the music industry, advertising, finance and as a paralegal? No. My prior experiences only enhance my value.

Yet, I would be lying if I said I never compared myself to others from time to time. There are people much younger than me who have seemingly achieved more success in a shorter period of time.

The only person you should compare yourself to is the one who looks back at you in the mirror. Measure your progress in terms of personal growth and development. Look at how much you've accomplished since you first picked up this book! I hope you refer to the "To Do" lists as a way to see how much closer you are to your landing your dream job or getting your dream project done.

Keep in mind that family and friends while often well intentioned don't know your process. They are not always familiar with the industry you want to make strides in and are not always supportive. Don't hold it against them. Instead immerse yourself with people who are on a path similar to yours.

THE ART OF THE PITCH

You may have heard a story about someone who pitched got their show picked up and was off and running in a short period of time. Much like in the game of baseball, I believe that the veracity, efficiency and outcome of the pitch are directly related to all of the preparation that takes place before you step up to that mound.

No matter what it looks like to you, every single person who has achieved some level of success has encountered opposition, delay and moments of insecurity. There is no such thing as an overnight success.

Just as you don't know the story behind the most successful people in the field you are seeking to enter, they don't know yours. Right now, in this moment, you have the ability to do something great. You have knowledge that others don't have. I knew nothing about pitching, television, protecting my work and so much more when I delivered my first pitch. I mentor several young people and marvel at how focused they are on achieving their goals.

I did not intentionally enter television. I "accidentally on purpose" landed a temp job after a period of disability that was preceded by me getting let go from a job. When we see people accepting awards for their achievements, we don't see their story - all we know is their glory.

I wrote this book so that others could have information that I never had as I started my television career. I don't have a college degree and I never went to film school. Experience has been my greatest teacher, yet I realize that just getting your foot in the door can be difficult and I hope this book helps in that regard.

Live your story, because every part of your life - personal, professional will become fuel for your pitch. Don't deny yourself of the advantages of process. Be intentional and that will get you where you are going much sooner.

Surround yourself with people who encourage and uplift you. It's important as you strive to do what no too many others are motivated to do: pursue your passion.

You can't see me, but I'm in the bleachers, cheering you on as you throw out that first pitch!

Additional Books in the Pro Series

Breaking Into Television:
An Insider's Guide

Do you want to pursue a career in television but
don't know where to start?

- ✓ Get answers to the following questions:
- ✓ Who does what on a television show?
- ✓ What should I expect my first day on set?
- ✓ When will I get to pitch my ideas?
- ✓ Where are all the jobs in television?
- ✓ Why is it so hard to break in?
- ✓ How can I contact a specific television or film crew?

www.breakingintotelevision.com

Opening Doors: Getting Connected

Have you ever wanted to get in touch with an influential person but don't know how?

Learn how to meet and develop relationships with those who often hold the key to your success and are able to walk you through doors you might not otherwise be granted access to. The principles are simple, practical and pertain to every career choice.

- ✓ Why You Need to Get Connected
- ✓ How To Use What You Know to Get What You Want
- ✓ Why You Should Offer Something of Value to a Valuable Person
- ✓ The Value of an Assistant's Assistance
- ✓ Why You Should Always Say Thank You and Mean It
- ✓ The Importance of Being Sociable

www.openingdoorsbook.com

Contact the Author

Author website

www.thatwritingchic.com

Follow the author on twitter:

@thatwritingchic

If you are interested in having the Author conduct a seminar, speak at an event or you would like a consultation, please email:

thatwritingchic@gmail.com